Color Your Own

DOLL'S HOUSE

Illustrated by
MARIA TAYLOR

STERLING CHILDREN'S BOOKS
New York

WELCOME TO 51 ORCHARD AVENUE

Down this tree-lined street, at number 51, is a beautiful Victorian house. Use colored pencils or pens to step back in time and decorate this doll's house. At the end of the book you can doodle and design your own house.

INSIDE THE DOLL'S HOUSE

This page shows you the whole of 51 Orchard Avenue, from the attic at the top, to the kitchen in the basement. You can color in the rooms like this, or use different colors. It's up to you!

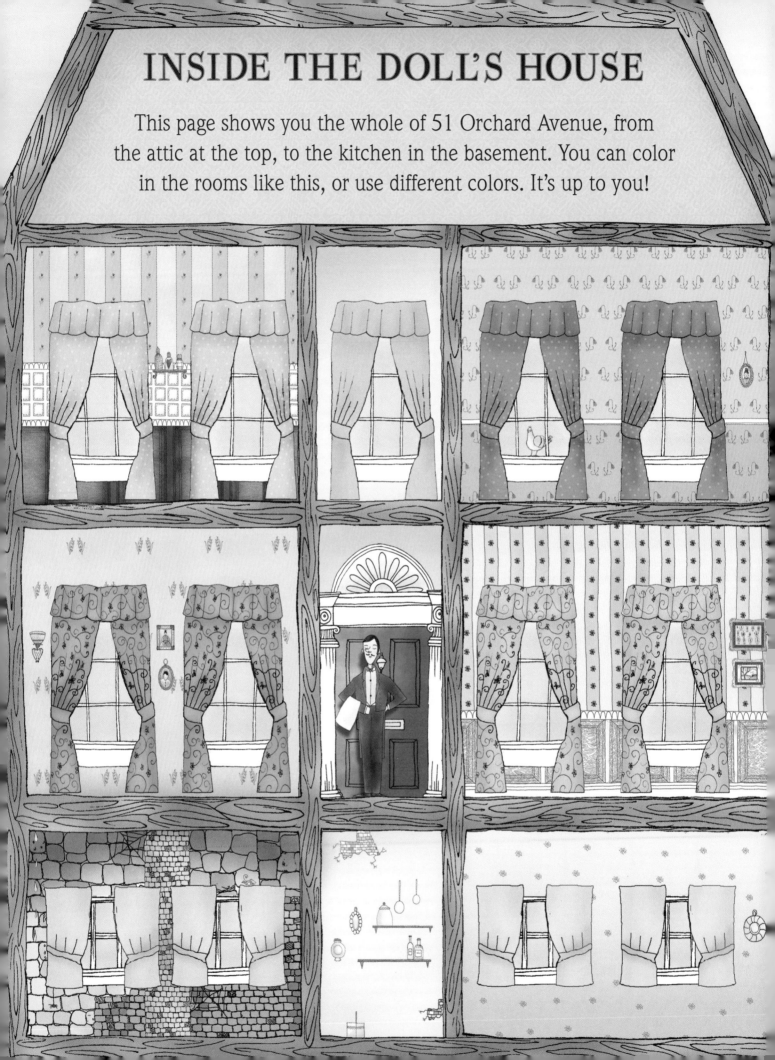

Nursery

Staff Quarters

Attic

Master Bedroom

Landing

Bathroom

Dining Room

Hallway

Drawing Room

Kitchen

Scullery

Cellar

MEET THE FAMILY

Mr. Sullivan

Mrs. Sullivan

Albert Sullivan

Rosie Sullivan

Matilda, the cat

Boots, the dog

The Sullivans are a wealthy family that live
here at 51 Orchard Avenue. The year is 1888.

Mr. and Mrs. Sullivan have two children,
Rosie, aged nine, and Albert, who is seven.
They also have a pet cat and dog
that are named Matilda and Boots.

THE STAFF

Mrs. King,
the cook

Mr. Parks,
the butler

Miss Porter,
the nanny

Ruby,
the maid

The butler, cook, nanny, and maid also live in
the house. There's always a lot going on—guests
coming for tea in the drawing room, children
playing in the nursery with their toys, and staff
cleaning the fireplaces and making the beds.

KITCHEN

It's incredibly busy in a Victorian kitchen! Pans bubble on the range—a big iron cooker heated by burning coal. When the cooking's done, the table is used for tasks like sewing, polishing shoes, and for the servants to eat their meals.

DRAWING ROOM

The drawing room is the prettiest room in the house. It is filled with grand furniture and is where Mr. and Mrs. Sullivan relax.

DINING ROOM

Isn't the dining room splendid?
Everyone dresses up for dinner.
Ladies wear gorgeous gowns and
gentlemen wear elegant suits.
The table is laid with sparkling
cutlery and beautiful china.

MASTER BEDROOM

The bed in Mr. and Mrs. Sullivan's bedroom is made of brass, with a mattress made from horsehair. It's covered with soft cotton sheets, heavy blankets, and a bedspread. Sometimes, a stone water bottle is put in the bed to warm it.

THE BATHROOM

Only the richest Victorians have
bathrooms. It's the latest fashion!
Most Victorians prefer to have a bath
in their bedroom in a tin tub.

THE NURSERY

Wealthy Victorian children like Rosie and Albert eat, play, and sleep in their nursery. They only see their parents in the morning and evening, and are looked after by a nanny.

STAFF QUARTERS

Right at the top of the house
is the attic, where the servants sleep.
It's cozy in winter and has a great view
in summer. The rest of the attic is
used to store old furniture and
other bits and pieces.

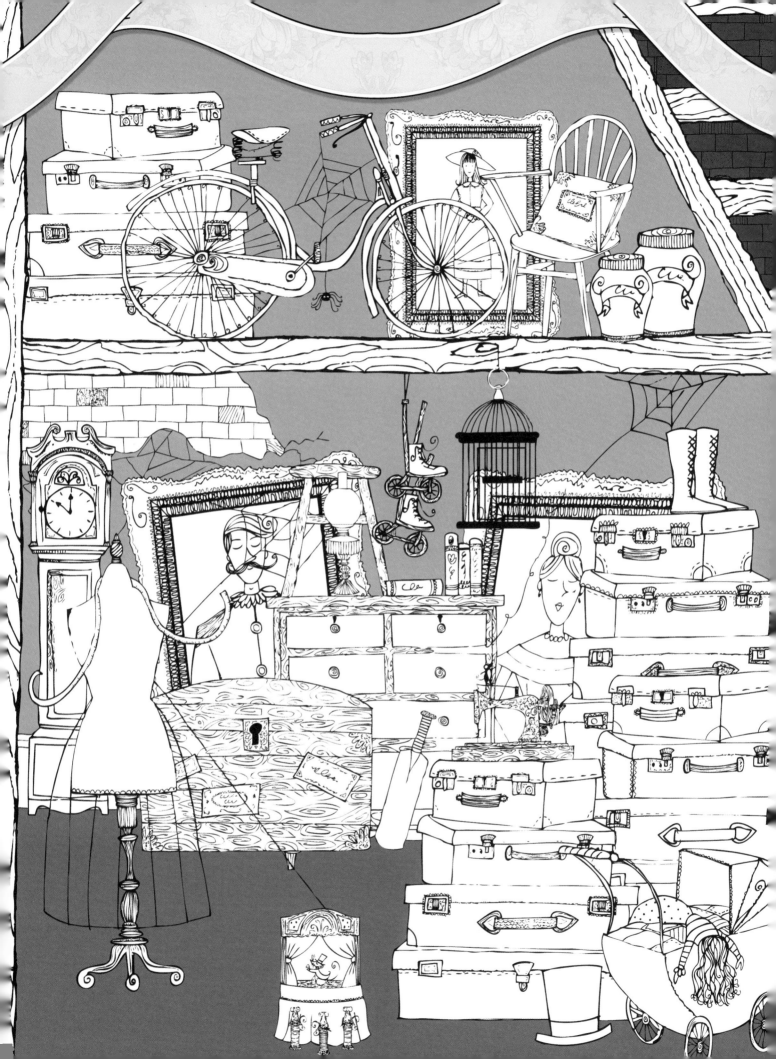

THE GARDEN

There is a beautiful garden at the back of the house that is blooming with flowers in the summer. Mr. Potts, the gardener, spends hours tending the garden.

WALKING DOWN THE STREET

It's all quiet along
Orchard Avenue today.
What do you think is going on
inside the other houses?

DOODLE TIME

Give the Sullivan family new outfits.
Don't be afraid to add patterns.

PLAN YOUR OWN HOUSE

Here is the plan of the house, but this time all the furniture has been removed. What do you think each room should be used for?

Write a name for each room in the purple panels. If you have a nursery, where would you put it—the bottom floor or the top? Where would you put your pets? Who would live at the top of the house?

Next, add some furniture to all the rooms. You could also draw in some wallpaper and pictures. Don't forget to add some people!

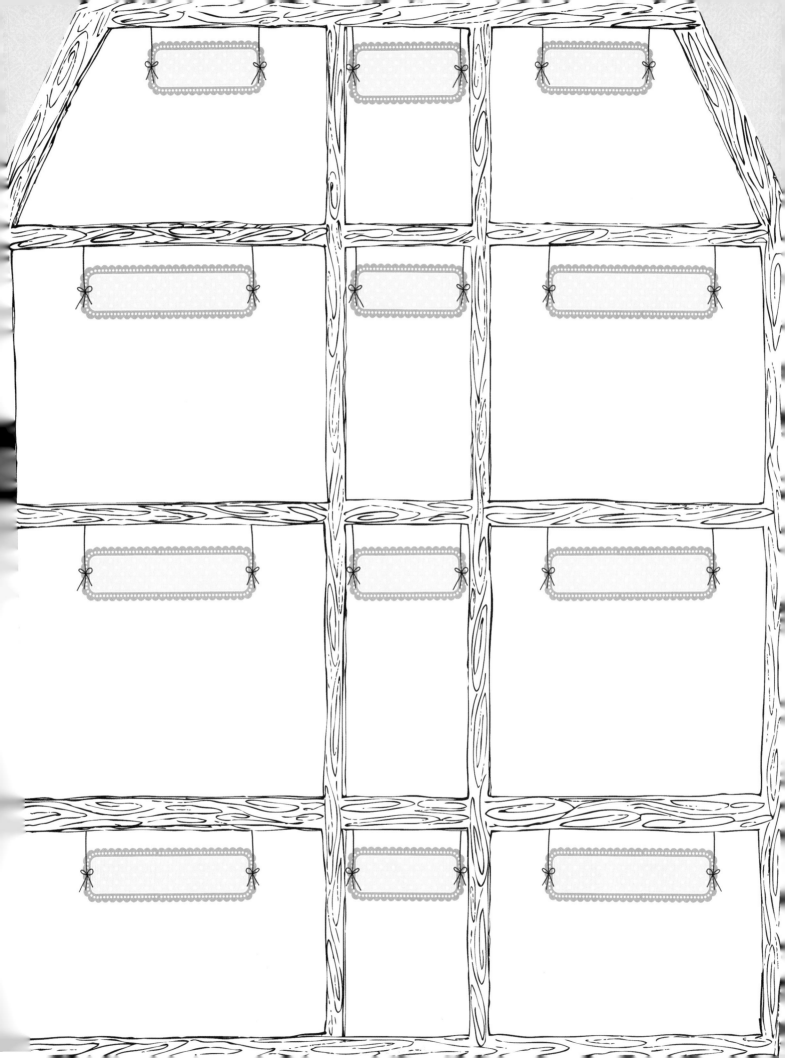

STERLING CHILDREN'S BOOKS
New York

An Imprint of Sterling Publishing
1166 Avenue of the Americas
New York, NY 10036

ISBN 978-1-4549-2222-3

Distributed in Canada by Sterling Publishing
c/o Canadian Manda Group, 664 Annette Street
Toronto, Ontario, Canada M6S 2C8
For information about custom editions, special sales,
and premium and corporate purchases, please contact
Sterling Special Sales at 800-805-5489 or
specialsales@sterlingpublishing.com.

Manufactured in China
Lot #:
2 4 6 8 10 9 7 5 3 1
08/16